Connell Short Guide
to
The reign of

———————

Queen Mary I

———————

by
Anna Neima

Contents

Introduction

Queen Mary I – or "Bloody Mary" as she's better known – ruled for only five years, from July 1553 to November 1558, and has a strong claim to being the most reviled monarch in English history. Echoing a widespread view, S.T. Bindoff calls her reign "politically bankrupt, spiritually impoverished, economically archaic, and intellectually enervated"; her failure to give birth to an heir has given licence to unkind jibes such as the historian A.F. Pollard's famous conclusion that "sterility was the conclusive note of her reign". Her reputation has been overshadowed by that of her much-eulogised half-sister Elizabeth: Mary is "the barren Catholic bigot who married an unpopular Spanish prince", while Elizabeth is "the Virgin Queen and a beacon of Protestant nationalism."[1] Mary's central policy – reviving "old world" Catholicism – has been condemned as an abject failure, "a mere hiccup" in the nation's triumphant and inevitable progress towards the "true religion" of Protestantism.[2] And on top of all that, her rule also saw the loss of Calais, England's last possession in continental Europe.

On the face of it that's an abysmal record, but recently a major salvage job has begun on Mary Tudor's reputation. The great achievement of her having gained the throne at all is increasingly being recognised. And rather than being dismissed as weak-willed and conventional, she has been re-evaluated by historians such as Judith Richards as a pioneer of female rule, a pathfinder to whom subsequent female monarchs (especially Elizabeth I) owed much. Scholars recognise that her government pursued coherent and generally well-thought-out policies, delivering many notable achievements in a very brief period, and even her strategy for restoring Catholicism is now looked at in a more positive light: if her reign had lasted any longer, England might well now be Catholic. "Bloody" Mary's poor historical reputation is as much down to bad luck as bad management: "by sheer misfortune she ran into the worst harvests and epidemics in the century and died before her work had any chance to take root".[3]

This brief survey presents the essential facts of her life and reign – from her upbringing, accession and marriage to her key policies, successes and failures as a ruler – taking in the conflicting views of historians along the way.

The turbulent early years

Mary's childhood was one of precarious dignity. Born on 18 February 1516 to Henry VIII and his first wife Katherine of Aragon, she was their first child to survive infancy. Henry was thrilled, and told the Venetian ambassador, "The Queen and I are both young, and if it is a girl this time, by God's grace boys will follow." While this hope lived, Mary was doted on, and she was well educated in the broad humanist Catholic tradition that characterised Henry's court in the 1520s and 30s.*

Her mother – the youngest daughter of Queen Isabella and King Ferdinand of Spain – took Mary's schooling seriously, and consulted the great Spanish humanist Juan Luis Vives for advice, commissioning him to write her a study plan and a treatise on the education of girls. The King, meanwhile, negotiated a series of potential marriages for her: she was promised first, aged two, to the Dauphin, the infant son of Francis I. A few years later she was instead contracted to her cousin, the 22-year-old Holy Roman Emperor Charles V, until he found a bride of childbearing age (his cousin Isabella of Portugal).

When she turned nine, Mary enjoyed a short spell as the *de facto* Princess of Wales (1525-1528).** Although she was never actually invested

*Christian humanism was the religious aspect of the Renaissance, a movement of cultural revival that sought inspiration from the classical past. Returning to the original texts of Christianity and seeking to reform the church in line with their teachings, it informed both Catholic and Protestant thought in the sixteenth century.

**The Princess of Wales is a courtesy title traditionally granted to the wife of the Prince of Wales, the heir apparent to the English throne. As Henry's intended successor, Mary was given many of the rights and properties usually conferred on the Prince of Wales, but she was never formally given the title.

3

with the title, she presided over her own household and was presented to the world as England's future sovereign. In these early years she was described as a pretty, precocious, lively girl who inspired deep affection in the women of her entourage and in her household officers.[4]

Unfortunately for Mary, this pleasant period was short-lived. Her mother could not oblige Henry in his desire for a male heir, and when the king began to address himself to solving that problem, Mary's life underwent a drastic change. She was traumatised by seeing her father first try to persuade the Pope to annul his marriage to her mother (on the basis that she was the widow of his brother and therefore unclean), and then rid himself of her in a divorce that also heralded the beginning of the English Reformation. He made himself "Supreme Head of the Church of England under Christ", annulled his own marriage and severed jurisdictional links to Rome.

During most of this period mother and daughter were kept apart. Katherine was banished from court. Mary's household was dissolved and she was sent in 1533, aged 17, to join the household of her new half-sister Elizabeth, daughter of Henry's second wife Anne Boleyn. Mary was deemed illegitimate and demoted from princess to "the lady Mary". She was often ill at this time, but in spite of her feeble state of health she showed the fiery stubbornness that would emerge as one of her chief characteristics by refusing ever to acknowledge Anne as queen. Henry was enraged, and he forbade her from seeing her mother as she was dying, or from attending her funeral in 1536.

After Anne was beheaded, Elizabeth too was declared illegitimate, and the two shared the burden of being cast out of courtly life. Henry's tender-hearted third wife, Jane Seymour, urged him to make peace with Mary, but the king insisted his daughter first accept him as supreme head of the church and admit the illegality of his marriage to Katherine. Mary tried to placate him by submitting to his authority, but only in so far as "God and my conscience" permitted. Ultimately, though, she was persuaded to sign a document agreeing to all his demands, including a declaration that her parent's marriage "was by God's law and man's law incestuous and unlawful". These were concessions that "would haunt her for the rest of her life" – but they allowed her to resume her place at court.[5]

The last decade of Henry's reign was easier on Mary. When Edward was born to Jane Seymour in 1537, Mary was made his godmother – a clear sign of her rehabilitation with the king. She acted as chief mourner when his mother died soon after. Although she was still treated as illegitimate, she reintegrated into life at court. She was particularly close to Henry's last wife Catherine Parr, with whom she shared a good humanist education and an interest in fashion. During the rest of Henry's reign there is very little evidence of what Mary's life was like, except in connection with a new series of marriage plans for her, taken up and then quickly abandoned. Her suitors included Duke Philip of Bavaria, who she found particularly repugnant because he was a Lutheran.* The climax of her years living in Henry's court came in 1544, when both she and Elizabeth were reinstated as heirs to the throne in the Act of Succession.

How did Catholic Mary fare under Protestant Edward VI?

On Henry VIII's death in 1547 his son Edward VI, aged nine, was too young to rule in person. The regency council that governed in his stead was dominated by religious reformers, bringing more storms for Mary. Where Henry had been content with breaking with Rome, authorising an English Bible and making limited Protestant doctrinal advances, Edward's councillors sought to complete the transition to full-blown Protestantism. Though Mary accepted her brother's right to succeed, she

* Lutheranism was launched in 1517 by the German cleric Martin Luther's efforts to reform the Catholic Church. Ultimately this resulted in a split from the Roman See, the development of a new branch of Protestantism and the spread of the Protestant Reformation across Europe.

quickly moved away from the royal court, enabling her to follow Catholic practice and to take control of the huge estates in Norfolk, Suffolk and Essex left to her by her father, making her one of the wealthiest landowners in the kingdom. Despite her detachment from the national religious question, she was naturally regarded with suspicion by the council as a potential focal point for opposition.

As Edward's reign progressed Mary came under increasing pressure to conform to the councillors' radical programme of reform. The Act of Uniformity of 1549 prescribed that all church services were to be held in English with fully Protestant rites. Mary remained defiant and increased the number of times the traditional Catholic Mass was celebrated in her household. Several of her household officers were imprisoned as heretics, but she herself was able to defy the council's new laws because of her wealth, her standing as heir apparent, and, most importantly, because Charles V – the most powerful man in Europe – set himself up as her protector, threatening war with England if Mary's religious liberty was curtailed.

When Mary attended a Christmas royal reunion with Elizabeth and Edward in 1550, the 12-year-old king reduced both himself and Mary to tears by publicly reproving her for ignoring his laws regarding worship. Nevertheless, she continued her dissent, and the king's council tried to sidestep the problem by marrying her off to a Protestant foreign power. Mary refused. From the safety of her vast estates, she wrote them a stern – and principled – no: "I would rather refuse the friendship of all the world . . . than forsake any point of my faith."

Mary's rise to power

Mary has gone down in history as weak, unimaginative and conventional, yet her ascent to the throne was nothing short of remarkable. C.S.L. Davies called it "the only successful rebellion in Tudor England" and Jennifer Loach "one of the

MARY IN PERSON

"She is of spare and delicate frame, quite unlike her father, who was tall and stout . . . When younger she was considered not merely tolerably handsome, but of beauty exceeding mediocrity. At present, with the exception of some wrinkles, caused more by anxieties than by age, which makes her appear some years older, her aspect, for the rest, is very grave. Her eyes are so piercing that they inspire not only respect, but fear in those on whom she fixes them . . . Her voice is rough and loud, almost like a man's, so that when she speaks she is always heard a long way off . . . "But whatever may be the amount deducted from her physical endowments, as much more may with truth, and without flattery, be added to those of her mind, as, besides the facility and quickness of her understanding, which most surprising events of the sixteenth century".

As the 15-year-old Edward lay dying in 1553, determined to safeguard his Protestant legacy, he declared that both his half-sisters were excluded from the throne since they were illegitimate. In a blatant refutation of Henry's Act of Succession, Edward turned to his cousin, Lady Jane Grey, and appointed her his heir. When he died, "few would have wagered positively" on Mary's chances of securing the throne.[6] She was a sickly woman exiled in the country with few declared supporters. On the other hand, almost all of Edward's leading advisers supported Jane. She was married to a son of the extremely powerful Duke of Northumberland (Lord President of the council

---

comprehends whatever is intelligible to others, even to those who are not of her own sex (a marvellous gift for a woman), she is skilled in five languages ...

"She is like other women, being sudden and passionate, and close and miserly, rather more so than would become a bountiful and generous queen ... whilst in certain things she is singular and without an equal, for not only is she brave and valiant, unlike other timid and spiritless women, but she is so courageous and resolute that neither in adversity nor peril did she ever even display or commit any act of cowardice or pusillanimity, maintaining always, on the contrary, a wonderful grandeur and dignity, knowing what became the dignity of a sovereign as well as any of the most consummate statesmen in her service."

Giovanni Michieli, the Venetian ambassador to Mary's court, 1557. ∎

during the later years of Edward's minority), and she unequivocally shared Edward's religious views. More importantly, her supporters controlled all aspects of the administration in London, and they had the support of the French – even Mary's greatest ally, the powerful Charles V, felt he could do nothing.

Jane was proclaimed queen. Yet her supporters fell short in one crucial respect: they failed to gain control of Mary. Secretly forewarned of Edward's fatal illness, she had fled to her East Anglian estates to rally her forces. This she did surprisingly quickly and effectively. Jane's supporters in London found that their political power meant nothing without the support of the masses – who turned their back on the Protestant clique in power in favour of Henry VIII's eldest daughter.

Mary entered the capital on the back of a groundswell of popular support on 3 August 1553. Historians debate how she managed this great feat. Most attribute it to the broad backing of the people – while some argue that this came from her perceived "legitimacy and legality", based in Henry's will and Act of Succession, others see it as chiefly motivated by religion. A third view is that, rather than mass popularity, it was the successful machinations of her faithful household retinue in exploiting the personal ties that Mary had gradually built up over her lifetime that enabled her to take the throne. Whichever way – and the

The Execution of Lady Jane Grey, *by Paul Delaroche, 1833*

truth is probably a combination of all three – Mary was proclaimed queen amid bonfires and ringing bells. Jane, now known as the "Nine Day Queen", was imprisoned in the Tower of London for high treason. Belying her bloody historical reputation, Mary initially spared her life. She was executed, however, after being implicated in Wyatt's rebellion of 1554.

Was Mary a pioneer of female rule?

Before 1553 there was only one serious attempt by a woman to rule England as queen regnant, and that was Matilda (c.1102-67), whose reign was marked by almost continuous civil war with her cousin Stephen. The received wisdom in Tudor England was that it was against the divinely ordained scheme for a woman to hold the reins of power, and Mary did not have an easy time asserting herself as regent. Historians have long seen her successor Elizabeth as the first to break this monarchical mould – England's iconic queen, she is hailed by A.F. Pollard as having triumphed in a male-dominated culture by being "more masculine than any queen in English history". Mary, on the other hand, is more often condemned as a "profoundly conventional woman".[7]

Recently, however, scholars such as Judith Richards have suggested that Mary deserves more credit than she's given, and a closer look reveals the considerable skill with which she pioneered a new model of queenship. She transcended her gender by projecting an image of a strong ruler with masculine attributes and feminine virtues combined. On her coronation, for example, she dressed as a queen consort but accepted all the regalia of a male monarch. She appeared at the end of the ceremony holding two sceptres: the "one of the King, the other bearing a dove which, by custom, is given to the Queen". This had never been done before.

Mary continued the tradition of the "royal touch", which was said to heal certain illnesses, despite arguments that a woman could not do so. She stood her ground in the face of critics and demonstrated that female monarchy was as sacred as male. She dressed richly, illustrating her understanding of the importance of magnificence in projecting royal power. When Thomas Wyatt raised a rebellion against her rule, she skilfully combined her masculine and feminine roles while

THE TERMS OF THE ACT FOR THE MARRIAGE OF QUEEN MARY TO PHILIP OF SPAIN, 1554

"This treaty greatly honours and benefits England. The prince shall enjoy, jointly, the style and honour of king. He shall happily help administer England, preserving its rights, laws, privileges and customs. The Queen shall have total control of all offices, lands and revenues, and grant them to natural born Englishmen. Sincere friendship with Spain will be happily established forever, God willing, to benefit their successors. Should no children be born and the queen die before him, he shall accept the lawful heir. The prince shall take no jewels abroad, nor ships, guns or supplies. He shall renew defences of the realm. By this marriage, England shall not be entangled in war, and the prince shall observe England's peace with France." ■

rallying Londoners to her support: "If a Prince may earnestly love her subjects as a mother loves her child, then be sure that I, your lady and mistress, love and favour you as tenderly." The rebellion was quashed. Without Mary breaking this new ground before her, Elizabeth's more celebrated rule might have been quite different.

The failed Spanish marriage

Love and war were the two areas in which the challenge of Mary's gender was most keenly felt. She has been deemed by historians to have failed in both fields: but she is perhaps most infamous for her unsuccessful union with the foreign prince Philip, son of Charles V. *

From the death of her mother onward, Mary had relied heavily on Charles V, and when she gained the throne, she was determined almost from the first to take up his suggestion that she

* The grandson of Ferdinand and Isabella, Charles V (1500-1558) ruled the Spanish Empire from 1516 and then Holy Roman Empire from 1516 until his voluntary abdication in favour of his brother, Ferdinand I (as Holy Roman Emperor), and his son, Philip II (as ruler of the Spanish Empire), in 1556. He withdrew into monastic life and died soon after. At the height of his power, his empire spanned nearly four million square kilometres and he was a leading opponent of the Protestant Reformation.

marry his son. She has been criticised for her "unpatriotic" allegiance to Charles, but this was an era in which dynastic family ties counted for as much, if not more, than national ones. Given her isolation from most Englishmen in positions of authority – especially under Edward VI's rule – it makes sense that she sought his guidance. Although Philip was eleven years her junior and had a son by a previous marriage, he was heir to vast European and New World territories, and, she was sure, would help her bring England back into the Catholic fold. Without question, he was "the most prestigious marriage partner available at the time".[8]

Unfortunately, the marriage was deeply unpopular among her subjects. It promised to throw England into the arms of Spain and to place its resources at the disposal of the son of the Holy Roman Emperor. The House of Commons petitioned Mary to consider marrying an Englishman instead – Reginald Pole and Edward Courtenay were put forward as alternatives with a good royal lineage, but Mary insisted on Philip and insurrections broke out in different parts of the country. Most of these fizzled out rapidly, since they failed to gather mass support. Thomas Wyatt, however, who regarded the "the queen's determinate pleasure to marry with a stranger" as an outrage on the nation's honour, successfully rallied a force of over 20,000 in Kent. He set out for London, determined to depose Mary in favour of Elizabeth.

The rebels had a number of successes, capturing royal ships at Gravesend, then Cooling Castle on the Thames Estuary, before marching into London. Mary's regime seemed to teeter on early extinction when government forces fled before their numbers. Disregarding her council's advice to leave the capital for her own protection, the queen addressed the citizens at the Guildhall – a steely speech that rallied support at the most crucial stage of the attack. More than 20,000 men enrolled for the protection of the city that night. Gradually Wyatt's numbers dwindled, and he finally surrendered.

Wyatt was beheaded, along with Lady Jane Grey, her father and her husband – all of whom were implicated in the conspiracy – and Elizabeth was put in the Tower of London for two months. Anti-Marian historians have represented this rebellion as an indicator of the fragility of her regime. Its quick suppression, however, can just as easily be read as a sign of her strength. Both her father and brother had experienced insurrections of a far greater magnitude, and took longer putting them down (under Henry, the Pilgrimage of Grace, 1536, and under Edward, the Prayer Book uprising, 1549).

In the event, the rebels' misgivings were at least partially confounded by Mary's engineering of a careful marriage treaty that "severely limited

Opposite: Philip II of Spain and Mary I of England by Hans Eworth, 1558

Philip's role while allowing her to continue in power as sovereign queen".[9] In England, under common law the property and titles belonging to a woman would become her husband's upon marriage. Mary, however, in another example of her shrewd combination of male strength and female virtue, forged a precedent thast would be followed by later queens: she drew a distinction between her private duty to her husband and the obligations of her public office. The marriage treaty named Philip as King and allowed his title precedence over hers, but it also confined his English role to that, effectively, of political wife – he could not act in England without her consent.

On the success of the marriage itself, historians are divided. The traditional view is to see it as a complete failure, with Mary fawningly dependent and Philip aloof but dominant. Philip was infuriated by the disadvantageous terms of the marriage treaty and unimpressed by the personal charms of his bride. He refused to learn more than a phrase of English and as soon as he could left England to command his armies against the French in the Low Countries (modern day Holland and Belgium), only returning for the short period of March to July 1557 in order to commit England to his war with the French. The fatal stroke was Mary's humiliating and much publicised false pregnancy. At the opening of parliament in November 1554 she appeared with "her belly laid out, that all men might see that she was with child". Festivities were held at court and the conception of the longed-for Anglo-Spanish heir was announced in a celebratory service at St Paul's Cathedral. Unhappily the hope proved unfounded.

Another school of scholars, including Alexander Samson, argue that the marriage was in many ways a great success. Samson presents Philip as likeable and pragmatic, Mary as independent and politically astute, and their union as a beacon of Catholic hope that was looked to throughout Europe. The influence Philip exercised in England is, in fact, very difficult to quantify: his English archives have been lost; anything he achieved was a matter of many delicate, unrecorded negotiations; and he spent more time out of England than in it. From the first, however, he was involved in governmental matters. The council's proceedings were translated into either Spanish or Latin for him to read, and he worked with Mary on the day-to-day aspects of her rule. Even after leaving for the Netherlands, he continued to be involved in allotting appointments and assignments.

The loss of Calais

In military terms, Mary's reign was undoubtedly a disaster. Whereas Elizabeth is invoked as the triumphant warrior queen who led victory against the Armada in 1588, Mary is remembered for losing Calais. The marriage settlement with Philip was specifically designed to prevent England being dragged into Spain's wars, and when Philip attempted to persuade Mary to support his fight against France, her council was resolutely opposed. However, an incident occurred which made England's entry into the war inevitable – Thomas Stafford, Reginald Pole's wayward nephew who had already previously been involved in Wyatt's rebellion again the Spanish marriage, landed in Scarborough with French help and took the castle there, proclaiming himself "Protector of England" and promising to return the throne to "the trewe Inglyshe bloude of our owne naterell countrye". Such provocation from the French could not be ignored.

From Mary's point of view the war had two very unfortunate outcomes. The first was the loss of Calais in January 1558, England's last possession on the European mainland. At this, she is said to have lamented: "When I am dead and opened, you shall find 'Calais' lying in my heart." The second was that Pope Paul IV took the part of Henry II of France in the conflict. In a cruel twist, the marriage that had been contracted to bring England back to the Holy See turned the queen into the Pope's enemy. Despite this double misfortune, the war itself was not as badly conducted as some historians have contended and the English defeat was quite largely attributable to an unprecedentedly cold winter. The watercourses that traditionally provided Calais with a natural defence against land attack froze over, allowing the French troops easy access. Had the queen lived longer, she probably would have seen her territory given back: Philip and Henry II were discussing the terms for peace, including the return of Calais, when Mary died.

The day-to-day of Mary's reign

The economic and social policies of Mary's reign – the more mundane, day-to-day politics of it – have traditionally been rolled up by historians such as Whitney Jones in the notion that there was a "mid-Tudor crisis" when pretty much everything went wrong. A closer examination, however, brings to light the administrative creativity of the Marian government, with genuine and successful efforts to meet problems as they arose.

Chief among Mary's accomplishments was the reform of the customs. The existing customs duties, one of the main sources of royal income, were outmoded and inflexible. In 1557 she convened a committee to analyse "why customs and subsidies be greatly diminished and decayed". The outcome was a new Book of Rates that

FIVE FACTS ABOUT
QUEEN MARY I

1. The Mother Goose nursery rhyme, *Mary, Mary, quite contrary* is said to be inspired by the monarch. The silver bells represent Catholic cathedral bells, the cockle shells, the pilgrimage to Spain and the pretty maids in a row, a row of nuns.

2. Despite Mary's sober and devout reputation, she took after her father in her fondness for gambling at cards. Her privy purse accounts show she lost considerable amounts of money this way from about 1537 to the end of her reign.

3. Mary and her half-sister Elizabeth I share a tomb in Westminster Abbey. James I relocated Elizabeth's body from a vault in the Abbey three years after her death. The Latin inscription on the monument reads: "Partners both in throne and grave, here we sleep Mary and Elizabeth, sisters in the hope of the Resurrection."

4. Elizabeth I has gone down in history as the great fashionista, but Mary too enjoyed fine clothes and jewels. The annual cost of the Great Wardrobe was £18,000 during the first years of her reign. It later fell to £6,000 – still on a par with Henry VIII's most extravagant last years.

5. The personal motto of Mary was *Veritas Temporis Filia* which translates as 'Truth, the Daughter of Time'.

Opposite: Portrait of Mary I at the Age of 28, 1544 by Master John

revaluated customs duties and broadened their scope. As a result, customs receipts were increased by 75 per cent. The Marian Book of Rates survived essentially unchanged until 1604.

In another impressive fiscal initiative, in order to restore a sound currency after several debasements under Henry and Edward, Mary's advisers devised the blueprint for a great recoinage. In the event, Mary died before it could be enacted, but it was adopted wholesale by Elizabeth, who "could never have tackled the problem of the coinage either so quickly or so effectively as she did had it not been so thoroughly aired" under Mary. [10]

Elsewhere, the government became more closely involved in economic regulation and institutional charity. The Retail Trades Act of 1554, for example, protected the retail monopoly of merchants from unregulated competition. And in response to the need for more systematised poverty relief, in London Mary's council presided over the welding of five leading charities into a citywide system of social welfare. Nationwide, the government undertook a systematic survey of grain stocks, punishing hoarders and ordering the distribution of grain where it was most needed.

The government's maintenance of order and improvements in effective administration becomes all the more impressive when considered against the adverse conditions that assailed the country during Mary's reign. In 1555 and 1556 heavy rain caused the worst harvest failures of the century. Straight afterwards, heavy mortality resulted from epidemics of typhus and influenza and may have helped reduce the population by up to 6 per cent between 1556 and 1561. Against this backdrop there was a costly war to be fought with France. There was certainly no significant improvement in the state of the economy or society under Mary, but in these "years of trauma" any state achievement above dogged survival was notable.[11]

The restoration of Catholicism: success or failure?

Mary wanted above all to return England to "that religion, which God and the world knoweth she hath ever possessed from her infancy hitherto". The traditional assessment of her drive for restoration was entirely negative. First, it was argued that Protestantism had spread spontaneously after the 1520s and was deeply and irreversibly ingrained among ordinary men and women. Second, that Mary's attempts to reverse this trend were uncreative, tyrannous and doomed to failure. While there were, in Catholic Europe, subsequent imaginative and successful efforts to put the Catholic house in order, Mary "failed to discover the Counter-Reformation".* Her restoration, after all, survived her by only a few months.

As with most things Marian, this interpretation has been challenged recently. In particular, the Irish historian Eamon Duffy has demonstrated that Mary's restoration of Catholicism was not an act inflicted from above on the unwilling people (as with the dissolution of the monasteries under Henry VIII), but a considerable part of her popular appeal. For the conservative majority, the worst aspect of Edward's reign had been "the assault on the Mass and the stripping away of an immemorial sacramental and ceremonial order". Much of the north and southwest remained resolutely Catholic throughout the reigns of Henry and Edward, and greeted the news of Mary's accession by the spontaneous restoration of the Latin Mass. The hallmark of her church was local enthusiasm, which allowed large sums of money to be raised quickly and to be spent on popular and rapid revival programmes. [12]

Eamon Duffy is also among the revisionist historians who now emphasise that the Marian

*The Counter-Reformation denotes a period of Catholic revival lasting from the middle of the sixteenth to the middle of the seventeenth century. Arising largely in answer to the Protestant Reformation, it focused on a strong affirmation of both the doctrine and structure of the Catholic Church.

restoration, far from being reactionary and conservative, was pioneering and inventive in its methods: a precursor to the widespread European movement for Catholic revival, it was "the closest thing in Europe to a laboratory for counter-reformation experiment". The combination of widespread initial popular support and a generally well-thought-out strategy for restoration meant that even within five years the traditional church regained much of the ground it had lost.

How did Mary re-Catholicise England?

Mary's first parliament of October 1553 passed a Statute of Repeal discarding most of the religious legislation passed during Edward's rule. A second Statute of Repeal in 1554 undid most of Henry's religious reforms, although, crucially, it did not touch the church lands that had been sold in the 1530s and 1540s – to have done so would have courted possibly insuperable unpopularity among those who had acquired them, and imperilled the regime.

Even before the first parliament, however, the queen's first priority was the return of the ceremonies and physical signs of the old faith. Churches that had been emptied of ornament and white-washed under Edward so that worshippers could concentrate on the word of God were now flooded with colour as altars, statues and painted windows were replaced. Saint days, craft processions, Corpus Christi plays and traditions such as morris dancing re-appeared. The emphasis laid by the Marian authorities on the physical and ceremonial aspects of the church has been criticised by some historians, who characterise her restoration as anti-intellectual and backward-looking. This, however, was only the start.

Mary's bishops were carefully chosen for their intellectual and pastoral calibre. Mary's Archbishop of Canterbury was Reginald Pole, and his Legatine Synod focused on bishops's key role in reform: they were to be resident, to lead "spare and frugal" lives, and to concentrate on good preaching

WHO WAS REGINALD POLE ?

Reginald Pole (1500-1558) was the queen's cousin. An opponent of Henry's divorce, he was an exile from England for twenty-three years. He lived in Italy, immersed in progressive Catholic scholarship, first as a student and then a papal servant, being made cardinal in 1536. In 1549 when Pope Paul III died, Pole came close to being elected as his successor. He was sent to England in 1554 as a legate by the new pope, Paul IV, to absolve the realm from its schism. He was then appointed as Mary's Archbishop of Canterbury.

Known as the "invisible man" of the Marian restoration for his quiet, and catechising. The Bishop of Durham instructed his dean and chapter to "sow the seed of the word of God... lest through lack of knowledge of the Law of God the flock of Christ perish by spiritual famine". Week by week the regime made effective use of great public pulpits like Paul's Cross in London to promote its cause. In the view of Jennifer Loach there is no reason to doubt that, given time, these methods would have achieved the same success in creating a strong Catholic country as those employed in the Counter-Reformation to reinvigorate faith in continental Europe.

* The Council of Trent met in three sessions between 1545 and 1563. Presided over the by pope, it was the single most important event in the renewal of Catholicism in the sixteenth century. It's significance lay both in its clarification of doctrine and its program of practical reform. It was key to strengthening and modernising the Church in the face of the Protestant Reformation.

legalistic style, Pole is increasingly understood to have been its single most influential figure.[13] He stiffened Mary's will to overcome the religious transformation started by her father and helped her to initiate a well-articulated agenda of Catholic revival that in many ways anticipated the measures instigated to reform the Catholic Church at the Council of Trent.*

When Pope Paul IV allied with the French in their war with Philip, Pole tried to convey to Mary how impolitic it would be to join her husband in his fight with Christ's vicar, but he could not prevail. In revenge, Paul IV cancelled Pole's legateship and recalled him to Rome. He refused to go and remained in England to his death. ∎

How did Mary treat religious dissenters?

Despite acquiring the nickname "Bloody Mary" for her execution of religious dissenters, the queen allowed some 800 English Protestants to emigrate to Frankfurt, Geneva and Zurich at the beginning of her reign, including John Foxe. From there they launched a barrage of anti-Catholic propaganda to which the regime had to respond. The Marian church has often been accused of losing this "battle of the books", but in fact the authorities were well aware of the opportunities offered by the printing press. They poured out devotional treatises, sermons, homilies and catechisms. Their methods in this area were "in many respects trail-blazing".[14]

Despite their efforts, Mary's reign has always been considered through "the prism of persecution".[15] Nothing has given it a worse reputation than the fate of the 284 men and women who were executed after the return to medieval heresy laws in late 1554. These included John Rogers, the author of Henry VIII's Great English Bible, and the so-called Oxford Martyrs: Hugh Latimer, Nicholas Ridley and Thomas Cranmer. The main source for the story of these deaths is John Foxe's *Actes and Monuments* (or *Book of Martyrs*), published in 1563 – it is, as one might imagine, highly biased.

Historians (especially Protestant ones) have

tended to take Foxe's book at face value, concluding that the example of the "Marian martyrs" strengthened the Protestant faith rather than weakening it. More recently, however, Eamon Duffy has re-examined this, arguing that the burnings were, in fact, not only effective but also broadly accepted by the people. A "formidable weapon against Protestantism", the burnings were meant to deter Protestants and deterred they were. Victims were given a trial – fair by the standards of the time – and offered the opportunity to recant. The death penalty for heresy was not uncommon in western Christendom in the 16th century, and many authorities turned to it in their struggle to suppress new theologies.

In less than a year from her succession, Elizabeth had undone all the Marian reforms. Yet in order to enforce her new religious settlement she had to displace hundreds of Catholics from the church and universities. These men provided the backbone of a recusancy that flourished into the 1580s, both in exile and in the rural areas and remoter provinces of England.* The survival of Catholicism well into Elizabeth's reign suggests that the Marian church was built on firm foundations.

* The Elizabethan term recusancy, coming from the Latin *recusare* (to refuse) was used to describe those who remained loyal to the Catholic Church and would not attend Anglican services.

Conclusion

On the morning of 17th November, 1558, soon after the elevation of the Host at a Mass celebrated in her sick-room, Mary died. That same evening, Reginald Pole also died, said to be victim of the same influenza epidemic. With the death of the queen and cardinal, so died the hope of a Catholic England.

Yet despite the indictments of historians through the centuries, "sterility" was not the conclusive note of Mary's reign. She is now emerging as "more rational, less bloody, less reactionary, less tyrannical" than ever before. [16] Her council governed the country with quiet efficiency, extending and centralising royalty authority and reforming its finances; though her marriage did not enormously aid her position, it was not unpopular enough to threaten stability; and her fruitful experiments in restoration brought about a strengthening of the Catholic Church. Mary firmly laid the groundwork for queens to come – from Elizabeth I to Elizabeth II. Her poor reputation in history is, by and large, "not the result of any mistakes which she herself had made, nor of any failure on the part of her government, but of the natural disasters of harvest failure and epidemic disease – and above all her own premature death".[17]

At Mary's funeral service John White, Bishop

of Winchester, praised Mary, saying she was "a king's daughter; she was a king's sister; she was a king's wife. She was a queen, and by the same title a king also." It is the last achievement that is perhaps her most impressive. She was an "important paradigm-breaker", the first English sovereign to model female monarchy. She demonstrated that a woman might rule in a deeply patriarchal society where no queen had ruled before.[18]

A SHORT CHRONOLOGY

1516 Mary born in Greenwich, London

1517 Protestant Reformation in Germany

1533 January 25 Henry VIII marries Anne Boleyn and is excommunicated by Pope Clement VII

1533 September 7 Elizabeth I is born

1534 King Henry VIII breaks with the Church in Rome and the Act of Supremacy is passed

1534 March 23 Act of Succession. Mary's title is reduced to Lady Mary and she is declared a bastard

1536 January 7 Catherine of Aragon dies at Kimbolton Castle

1536 May 19 Queen Anne Boleyn is executed

1536 May 30 Henry VIII marries Jane Seymour

1537 Jane Seymour dies after the birth of a son, the future King Edward VI

1540 January 6 Henry VIII marries Anne of Cleves. The marriage is annulled six months later

1540 July 28 Henry VIII marries Catherine Howard

1542 February 13 Catherine Howard is executed

1543 July 12 Henry VIII marries Catherine Parr

1547 January 28 Henry VIII dies and Edward VI is pronounced King

1553 July 6 Edward VI dies

1553 July 10 Lady Jane Grey proclaimed Queen of England

1553 July 19 Lady Jane Grey deposed. Mary finally takes the crown as Queen of England

1554 February 12 Lady Jane Grey is executed at the Tower of London. Protestant rebellion, led by Sir Thomas Wyatt the Younger

1554 March 18 Princess Elizabeth is confined to the Tower of London

1554 May 19 Princess Elizabeth released from the Tower of London

1554 July 25 Mary marries King Philip of Spain. England forced to return to Roman Catholicism

1555 Accepts Princess Elizabeth as heir to the throne. Philip II leaves Mary and returns to Spain.

1558 November 17 Queen Mary I dies at St James's Palace, London. She is buried at Westminster Abbey

ENDNOTES

1. Alice Hunt and Anna Whitelock, *Tudor queenship: the reigns of Mary and Elizabeth* (2010)

2. Jennifer Loach, *Parliament and the crown in the reign of Mary Tudor* (1986)

3. Michael Hutchings, 'The Reign of Mary Tudor – A Reassessment', *History Today*, Issue 33 (March 1999)

4. Diarmaid MacCulloch, *The later Reformation in England, 1547-1603* (2001)

5. John Edwards, *Mary I: England's Catholic Queen* (2011)

6. Diarmaid Macculloch, *Ibid.*

7. David Loades, *The reign of Mary Tudor: politics, government and religion in England, 1553–58, 2nd edn* (1991)

8. Judith Richards, *Mary Tudor* (2008)

9. Sarah Duncan, *Mary I: gender, power and ceremony in the reign of England's first queen* (2012)

10. Christopher Edgar Challis, *The Tudor Coinage* (1978)

11. David Loades, *Ibid.*

12. Professor Haigh, *English Reformations: Religion, Politics and Society under the Tudors* (1993)

13. Eamon Duffy, *Fires of Faith: Catholic England under Mary Tudor* (2010)

14. Jennifer Loach, *The mid-Tudor polity, c.1540–1560* (1980)

15. Paulina Kewes, 'The Exclusion Crisis of 1553 and the Elizabethan Succession' in *Mary Tudor: Old and New Perspectives edited by Susan Doran and Thomas S. Freeman* (2011)

16. Judith Richards, *Mary Tudor* (2008)

17. David Loades, *Ibid.*

18. Susan Duncan, *Ibid.*

FURTHER READING

Sarah Duncan, *Mary I: gender, power and ceremony in the reign of England's first queen* (2012)

Alice Hunt and Anne Whitelock (eds.), *Tudor queenship: the reigns of Mary and Elizabeth* (2010)

Eamon Duffy, *Fires of Faith: Catholic England under Mary Tudor* (2010)

Jennifer Loach, *Parliament and the crown in the reign of Mary Tudor* (1986)

Jennifer Loach and Robert Tittler (eds.), *The mid-Tudor polity, c.1540–1560* (1980)

David Loades, *The reign of Mary Tudor: politics, government and religion in England, 1553–58,* 2nd edn (1991)

Diarmaid MacCulloch, *The later Reformation in England, 1547-1603* (2001)

Judith M. Richards, *Mary Tudor* (2008)

Notes

Notes

First published in 2016 by
Connell Guides
Artist House
35 Little Russell Street
London WC1A 2HH

10 9 8 7 6 5 4 3 2 1

Picture credits:
p.11 Public domain image
p.17 Public domain image
p.23 Public domain image

A CIP catalogue record for this book is available from the British Library.
ISBN 978-1-911187-28-8

Design © Nathan Burton
Written by Anna Neima

Assistant Editors and typeset by
Paul Woodward & Holly Bruce

www.connellguides.com

Printed and bound by CPI Group (UK) Ltd, Croydon, CR0 4YY